AF328485

Russia: The 1998 Crisis and Beyond

Kalin Nikolov was born in Russe, Bulgaria, and emigrated to Britain in 1990. He is the Research Officer at the Centre for Post-Collectivist Studies and holds a BA in Politics, Philosophy and Economics and an MPhil in Economics, both from The Queen's College, Oxford.

Russia:

The 1998 Crisis and Beyond

KALIN NIKOLOV

The Social Market Foundation
Centre for Post-Collectivist Studies
March 1999

First published by The Social Market Foundation, 1999

The Social Market Foundation
11 Tufton Street
London SW1P 3QB

ISBN 1 874097 429

Contents

Acknowledgements

I am greatly indebted to Robert Skidelsky for his invaluable comments and suggestions on the numerous drafts of this paper. I would also like to thank Mark Harrison for very helpful comments on an earlier version. The usual disclaimers apply.

'[The state]….. interferes in the economy where it shouldn't, while where it should, it does nothing.'

President Boris Yeltsin, 1997

1. Russia in Turmoil

Post–communist political and economic life in Russia has never been smooth and predictable. The spectre of impending crisis was always in the air during the past seven years that saw the collapse of the Soviet Empire, two unsuccessful coup attempts, brief flirtation with hyperinflation and the highly humiliating and bloody military conflict in Chechnia. The recent collapse of the fifth macroeconomic stabilisation attempt was no less dramatic and surprising to those who are not used to the constant twists and turns of events in the Russian Federation. In a matter of weeks the exchange rate collapsed from its peg at $1 = 6 Rbl to over 20 Rbl. The state has effectively defaulted on its debt obligations, thus inflicting billions of dollars of losses on reckless foreign and domestic investors, who disregarded the risks, enticed by the high returns on Russian government debt. Increasingly pessimistic observers have already begun to speak of Russia's 'lost decade'.

This excessive gloom is misguided. The lurches of economic policy during the transition period need to be seen in the context of the enormous economic and psychological shocks caused by the disintegration of a country, an economic system and a way of thinking. It is not easy to have to face up to the fact that 75 years of building 'real socialism' were in reality a wasted 'short century' in pursuit of utopian goals.

The current crisis is the latest hard lesson to be forced on to the tired people of the Russian Federation. Despite the advances in the conduct of monetary policy since 1992, budget balance was never achieved, and tough decisions were postponed continually until it became too late. The 1998 currency crisis was fiscal in origin and its solution also lies in the government learning to spend whatever its citizens and firms are willing to pay in taxes. This gives politicians a choice: either boost revenue collection and have a relatively large modern state or accept very limited government provision coupled with a limited tax intake. As recent events have demonstrated, ballooning public sector debt is not a long term option.

In the short term there is certainly very little ground for optimism. All the indications are that Russia is entering a period of denial and paralysis – an all-encompassing crisis with a political and constitutional as well as an economic dimension. How the crisis will unfold is uncertain and much depends on it. There will be an opportunity for the Russian political system to reinvent itself and throw away the old constraints (although the danger is there that it will be burdened with new ones). Already the press is brimming with rumours of the imminent demise of the 'financial oligarchy', whose corrupt backroom dominance of the policy making process during the late Yeltsin years is being blamed for the current crisis. A genuine unblocking of the political system could allow some more pieces of the stabilisation jigsaw to fit into place, namely the potential for long-overdue fiscal reform, which has been the stumbling block of all the recent stabilisation attempts.

The following pages outline some basic principles of stabilisation policy, and trace out Russia's attempts to achieve macroeconomic stabilisation, culminating with the recent successes and failures. I describe the origins of the current fiscal crisis and offer some (necessarily speculative) predictions about the immediate future of the political system and the economy.

2. The Anatomy of Crisis: The Rouble crash of 1998

1997 will probably be remembered as an exceptionally good year for the Russian economy. Having opened the treasury bill (GKO) market to overseas investors, the Chernomyrdin government was reaping the rewards of its new found monetary orthodoxy as increasing confidence at home and abroad was driving bond yields to new lows and finance was flowing into the economy. The balance of payments was in healthy surplus, the real exchange rate was remarkably stable while the central bank

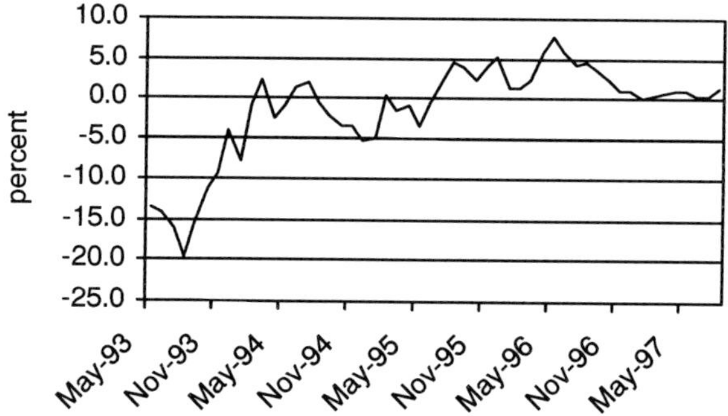

Figure 1: Real Monthly GKO Yields
Source:Russian Economic Trends

was experiencing an increase in foreign reserves[1] and the economy was at long last beginning to recover.

The high level of public borrowing, however, remained the most significant black spot on the horizon. The budget deficit was 7.8% in 1996 and 7.2% in 1997, and was almost exclusively financed by GKO/OFZ[2] emissions. Given the high real interest rates in Russia (see Figure 1) and the negative rates of economic growth during this period, bond sales on such a scale were leading to a rapid growth of the stock of debt relative to GNP (see Figure 2). Although this was not very high compared to other emerging markets, the speed with which it was growing should have caused alarm among investors. At the time, however, confidence in the new found effectiveness of the Russian government to deal with pressing economic issues was riding high following the success of its recent stabilisation attempt.

Indeed, the actions of the Chernomyrdin administration since 1994 provided some grounds for such faith. The primary fiscal balance (the budget deficit excluding interest payments) had come down from 10.4% of GDP in 1994 to 3.3% in the 1995-97 period, which represents a huge tightening of the state finances. As the continuing fiscal shortfalls were the result of poor tax collection and high interest payments on the national debt,

---

[1] The CBR's reserves, however, did not rise by as much as anticipated. A systematic swing of the 'errors and omissions' component of the Balance of Payments figures into negative territory (which some economists argue indicates illegal capital flight) suggests that Russians may have begun to take their money out of the country illegally as early as 1994.

[2] Rouble denominated Russian government bonds.

international investors reasoned that a rapid recovery, a fall in interest rates, and concerted efforts by the government to boost tax revenues would alleviate a state liquidity crisis. Such reasoning turned out to be wrong. A mixture of global and domestic factors conspired to bring about the fall of the rouble's parity against the dollar, the political crisis that ensued, and the end of this period of unprecedented economic stability.

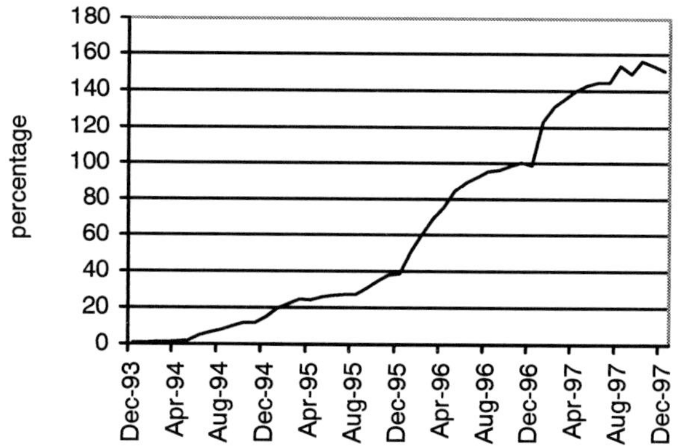

Figure 2: Nominal GKO/OFZ stock as percentage of monthly GDP
Source: Russian Economic Trends

The first such shock was the Asian crisis, which shook world financial markets and reminded investors of the inherent dangers of 'exotic' debt and equity. Shifting risk perceptions led to substantial capital outflows as early as the final quarter of 1997. The government managed to save the day by a mixture of interest rate hikes, exchange market intervention and a switch from rouble-denominated GKO/OFZs to dollar-denominated Eurobonds. However, as reserve levels were limited and the national debt stock was growing rapidly at the higher interest rates, a fiscal retrenchment was desperately needed in order to meet the huge GKO/OFZ and Eurobond redemptions falling due in late 1998 and 1999.

In a highly promising move, President Boris Yeltsin suddenly reminded observers of his still strong grip on power by sacking his prime-minister Victor Chernomyrdin in March 1998 and appointing a little known economist named Sergei Kirienko to head the government. The move was designed to strengthen the hand of the reformers and ensure that much needed fiscal reforms would be pushed through the Duma. Improving tax collection was at the top of the policy agenda. The increasingly difficult international environment meant that large primary surpluses were required for the continued servicing of the national debt without resorting to the printing press.

The strategy pursued by the government was to put pressure on the state owned gas and oil monopolies, which had an enormous backlog of unpaid taxes and dividends to the state. A public stand off between the cabinet and Gazprom, the privatised gas monopoly, followed in July 1998, with the final result seen largely as a Gazprom victory. Although the gas monopoly agreed to increase tax payments by up to Rbl 2 billion per month, this fell far short of what the company actually owed to the treasury. The weakness in the government's bargaining position arose mainly from the fact that Gazprom itself was suffering from non-payment by industrial customers. Hence, faced with a tax bill from the cabinet on the basis of total gas deliveries rather than the payment for them, the company threatened to cut off the gas supplies of its debtors. Such an outcome was unacceptable to the government, which backed down from its initial demands[3].

A further deterioration in the macroeconomic situation in 1998 was brought about by the Asian crisis-induced fall in oil prices. Since Russia is a major net oil exporter (crude petroleum comprised 47.4% of its total exports in 1997), this negative terms of trade shock had several adverse effects on the domestic economy. As demand for oil is very inelastic, the fall in oil prices reduced export revenues and sent the current account into an annualised deficit of $4 billion for the first time since 1992. Secondly, lower profits for the oil companies (who are some of the few Russian firms who actually make profits) meant that they paid even fewer taxes, further worsening the financing problems of the government. Adding to its real effect on the economy, the fall in oil prices contributed to the financial market panic, forcing up interest rates on GKOs and leading to more haemorrhaging of foreign exchange reserves.

At the same time the weakness of the Russian financial sector constrained the government in its use of monetary policy to defend the rouble. Overleveraged and overexposed to the GKO market, the Russian banking sector was beginning to suffer from liquidity problems as

---

[3] See further discussion of the causes and consequences of this mass non-payment in Chapter 3.

bond prices fell and the monetary base shrank. Increasing numbers of observers were beginning to express deep reservations about the ability of the banking system to survive a crash of the rouble, which further undermined the market's confidence in the currency. According to *Komersant Daily* in July 1996, Russia's financial institutions had \$19.2 billion in debts to foreign creditors, of which at least \$1 billion was to be repaid within the following three months. Furthermore the banks were exposed to an uncertain amount of forward foreign exchange contracts, which would realise substantial losses in the event of a rouble devaluation. Such factors served to deepen the financial panic as well as to undermine the authorities' ability to respond adequately. Despite a \$22.7 billion IMF loan on 13 July 1998, foreign currency reserve loss continued at the unsustainable pace of up to \$1 billion per week. By early August, it became clear that further attempts to prop up the rouble would lead to the collapse of the financial system. The CBR began lending to troubled banks through the discount window only to find the funds being sold on the foreign exchange market contributing to more erosion of reserves. Finally the monetary authorities bowed to market pressure and announced a *de facto* 33% devaluation of the Russian currency on August 17. The exchange rate breached the new trading band almost immediately falling to \$1=Rbl 25, before recovering somewhat since.

The devaluation was followed by the introduction of stringent exchange controls to stop capital flight, as well as the 'restructuring' of the internal debt (the rouble denominated GKOs), which constituted a *de facto* default on the sovereign debt. The current arrangements regarding the GKO/OFZ bonds include a three month moratorium on all payments (which has now expired although no agreement has been reached), as well as a voluntary scheme whereby investors can convert the short maturity GKOs for long term dollar denominated securities (with seven and twenty year maturities). The total outstanding stock of debt is approximately $47 billion of which foreign investors hold at least $10 billion. At present the secondary market value of the Russian government securities has fallen to less than 3 cents in the dollar, implying a lack of faith by bond holders that the state will soon settle its obligations in full.

The August devaluation and debt default mark the end of three years of serious albeit incomplete reform efforts by the Russian state, which brought inflation under control for the first time since the start of the transition. Currently Russia is in the grip of a serious political *impasse* as neither the reformers nor the Communists appear capable or willing to govern alone. The fiscal deterioration of the last seven years has turned into a collapse as even the meagre revenue which the federal government was able to collect has now dried up and many functions of the state have ground to a halt. The threats by a desperate Primakov administration to finance its expenditure commitments by printing money brings closer the threat of very high inflation (possibly even hyperinflation) and dark times for the Russian economy and its impoverished people.

The rest of this paper charts out the reform efforts of the Russian state since its inception in 1992 and stresses the fiscal strains which have been an endemic feature of transition. It is these strains and in particular the collapse in the government's capacity to collect tax revenues which lies behind Russia's inability to achieve lasting macroeconomic stabilisation.

3. Lessons in Monetarism: the early reform efforts of 1992–1996

The collapse of the Soviet Union following the 1991 coup brought chaos to an already disintegrating command economy. The government was losing control of the macroeconomy as a result of the botched reform efforts of the Gorbachev years. Severe supply disturbances due to foreign exchange shortage, collapse of CMEA[4] trade, loss of budgetary control and extreme political uncertainty were bringing a vicious circle of falling output, rising fiscal deficit and explosive excess demand at official prices. In 1991 real GDP fell by 15% while the state budget deficit surged to a staggering 16% of national output (financed exclusively by money creation). By the time the decision to embark on the road to capitalism was taken, Russia was in a very difficult economic situation, which necessitated radical and decisive action to prevent a degeneration into complete chaos. The following years were a rollercoaster of serious reform efforts followed by lapses of resolve and renewed attempts at stabilisation.

Transitional inflation and the early stages of the fiscal collapse

Much has been written on the causes of the early inflation in post-communist economies. The shortages of

---

[4] CMEA (Council for Mutual Economic Assistance) was the trading organisation of the Communist block.

the Soviet era had led to the accumulation of 'forced savings' and 'forced substitution', whereby households failed to attain their desired consumption patterns and either 'saved' the excess money balances or spent them on available goods. Upon liberalisation of prices the severe disequilibrium caused an initial price jump, which, it was thought, would clear the market.

There is always a danger, however, that such a situation may get out of control and degenerate into hyperinflation as state revenues collapse rapidly in the chaotic early years of transition while powerful special interests demand that the state maintains their 'real'[5] incomes in the face of inflation. Unless there exists a political consensus regarding the need for macroeconomic stabilisation and the share of the costs to be borne by different groups in society, the budgetary retrenchment process can be painfully slow, while increasingly large fiscal imbalances are filled by exploding quantities of central bank credit (i.e. money printing). Such dangers are particularly serious in developing economies which cannot attract non-inflationary bond finance and have to rely exclusively on *seigniorage* to fund their deficits.

A frequently cited argument for this kind of inflationary deficit finance is that it acts as a form of Keynesian short term demand management. Although it leads to high inflation, the argument goes, in its absence there would be an even deeper output collapse with enormous social costs.

---

[5] Of course in a shortage economy the notion of 'real income' is not a straightforward one precisely because official prices were not realistic.

This reasoning rests on a fundamental misunderstanding about the different causes of developed economy recessions on the one hand and transitional recessions on the other. In developed market economies there are occasional episodes of consumer and investor pessimism which lead to excessive 'liquidity preference' (i.e. excess demand for the safest asset – money) and hence insufficient investment and consumption for the maintenance of full employment. What follows is a fall in output and employment further feeding the pessimism of market actors and leading to a business cycle downturn. Hence the government must increase the supply of money to satisfy people's temporary desire to hold more of it and borrow and spend on goods and services as a 'purchaser of last resort'.

What is crucial here is that, first of all, the government *can* raise the taxes to pay for its extra spending but it chooses not to do so in order to increase the level of aggregate demand in the economy. Secondly, the insufficient demand for goods and services develops due to a failure of the market to adjust immediately. Given time, the price mechanism would ensure that supply is equal to demand for both goods and money.

The Russian situation was (and is) very different. At the outset of transition there was *excess demand* for goods and an excess supply of money at prevailing prices – the exact opposite of classical recessions. The reason why output fell as the general price level rose therefore had very little to do with a Keynesian slump. Its explanations instead centre on the supply disturbances caused by the end of the command system and on the low quality of output, which could not be sold at a price that covered inefficient enterprises' inflated production costs.

Hence deficit spending and the resulting high monetary emissions in Russia during 1991-1995 had little to do with the Keynesian case for demand management but rather reflected the collapse of the state's capacity to collect revenues to cover even its basic functions. At the same time, money was pumped into enterprises which were unviable at any level of aggregate demand. Thus the evolution of the rate of inflation reflected the state's seigniorage needs and the public's willingness to pay 'the inflation tax' by holding domestic currency.

What needs to be done in order to stabilise the economy is to deal with the cause of monetary growth (*the orthodox method*). This is almost invariably the budget[6] and hence disinflation is impossible unless either the state finds alternative means of budgetary financing to seigniorage (tax rises, spending cuts, bond sales[7] or improved revenue collection[8]) or cut expenditure itself. What is needed for this is political consensus on the need for budgetary reform and on the means of carrying it through.

Credibility is essential in ensuring a speedy and (relatively) costless stabilisation. Transition economy experiences suggest that fixing the nominal exchange rate

---

[6] Although it can be caused by the private sector excesses.

[7] Switching from inflationary to bond finance can of course lead to *higher current inflation* through Sargent and Wallace (1981) style 'unpleasant monetary arithmetic'. Inflation will only fall if the private sector expects a future fiscal retrenchment in order to service the higher bond stock.

[8] In most CIS economies it is low tax take rather than low tax rates which are at the root of the fiscal problem.

is the most effective method of achieving this and ensuring rapid disinflation at minimum output cost[9] (*the heterodox method*). Examples abound of hyperinflationary spirals being brought under control in a matter of months by credible and decisive stabilisation programmes involving fixed exchange rates. By far the most effective route seems to be the imposition of a currency board regime[10] as practised by Bulgaria and Estonia.

Note, however, that Russia's unsuccessful stabilisation attempts failed because their architects relied excessively on heterodox means of disinflation and paid insufficient attention to the underlying monetary (and budgetary) causes of the inflationary process (see next chapter). Again the direct implication of this fact for the likely success of current attempts of the Primakov government to print money while maintaining stability through exchange controls and incomes policies, should be clear.

A chronology of stabilisation attempts in Russia: 1992-1996[11]

The Gaidar government undertook the first Russian stabilisation effort in January 1992. It liberalised prices and the severe repressed inflation of the Gorbachev years manifested itself in a spectacular overnight price jump

---

[9] See Bruno (1992) for a discussion of the advantages of using heterodox elements in disinflation programmes.

[10] See later discussion regarding the use of such a policy in Russia.

[11] For a more complete discussion of the early reform efforts, see Skidelsky and Halligan (1996).

of 350%. The Gaidar programme constituted sharp subsidy cuts, which amounted to 15% of GDP in 1991 and military procurement reductions of up to 70%. He also imposed value-added tax at 28%, since this was considered more easily collectable than direct taxation. On the monetary side, Gaidar imposed stringent reserve requirements on banks in order to reduce their lending and ensure their stability. These efforts were initially effective in slowing money supply (M2) growth and bringing inflation down to 9% per month by August 1992. However, the government's resolve to impose financial discipline did not hold and large amounts of credit were extended by the central bank to state owned enterprises throughout the former Soviet Union, in order to ease domestic liquidity shortages and stimulate CIS demand for Russian goods. This led to a surge in the budget deficit and hence in M2 growth which rose to 28% a month in the third quarter. By the end of the year, Gaidar's programme lay in tatters as the annualised inflation rate reached 1354% in 1992 according to official data from the central bank[12].

Russia's first stabilisation effort failed for the simple reason that the government failed to control the budget deficit and consequently the money supply. Attempts to maintain trade links with other CIS republics and to clear inter-enterprise payment arrears by issuing large amounts of soft rouble credits were some of the direct causes of this failure. Another was the lack of an explicit and credible currency stabilisation plan.

The deeper and more fundamental reasons, however, lay in the political climate in Russia in 1992,

---

[12] IMF estimates actually put it at over 2000%.

which was far from a consensus on the need for a stabilisation. There was enormous pressure on the government from the communist-dominated parliament and the industrial lobby to relax its tough monetary stance and bail out loss-makers. In the end, Yeltsin and Gaidar had to compromise and abandon their 'shock therapy' programme.

The great reformist survivor of Russian politics, Boris Fyodorov, masterminded the next stabilisation attempt in 1993. He cut off the former Soviet republics from Russian Central Bank (CBR) credit and imposed domestic credit ceilings. The government succeeded only in its first objective. Strong political pressure for subsidies resulted in higher credit emissions than the published targets, with the annual volume of CBR credit reaching 10% of GDP. Thus, lack of programme credibility and fiscal control led to rapid M2 growth and surging money velocity,[13] which in turn brought about a very high annual inflation rate of 890% in 1993.

After the failed Rutskoi-Khasbulatov coup attempt, the Chernomyrdin government embarked on a new stabilisation effort in 1994. A system of credit ceilings was imposed to directly restrict the money supply as well as setting the CBR refinancing rate at penal levels in order to discourage commercial bank borrowing from the central bank. Like its two predecessors, this stabilisation attempt fell victim to lack of political resolve to stop inflationary

---

[13] Money velocity is the ratio of nominal income to the money stock. Sharp increases in this ratio are generally indicative of the public's unwillingness to hold domestic currency for instance because of high inflationary expectations.

budget deficit financing and/or close the fiscal gap altogether. State demand for credit alone accounted for a monetary expansion of the order of 10% of GDP in the second half of 1994. Unsurprisingly, by the end of the same year, monthly inflation was back to double digits.

Table 1: Money, Credit and Inflation: 1991 – 1997

Year	1991	1992	1993	1994	1995	1996	1997
Budget Deficit	31	18.8	7.6	10	5.7	7.2	7.8
Credit to Government	127	803	452	242	4	n.a.	n.a.
M2 Growth	126	643	416	192	126	31	28
Inflation	92.7	1354	874	307	197	48	15

Source: Russian Central Bank.

The only successful stabilisation programme (albeit for a limited period of time) was started by Chernomyrdin and Chubais in 1995. It is so far the only relatively comprehensive attempt to deal with the macroeconomic situation, involving explicit targets for key variables such as the currency as a means of gaining market confidence.

For the first time attention was paid to the central bank's balance sheet (Net Domestic Assets) as a means of stabilising monetary conditions and the exchange rate. The CBR stopped buying government bonds and issuing credit to state enterprises (which is, in effect, printing money) while an explicit fiscal deficit target of 5.6% of GDP was adopted. Initially interest rates rose sharply as the government began financing up to two-thirds of its borrowing needs from private domestic residents[14]. Subsequently, shifting market sentiments regarding the prospects for reform brought about a decline in both nominal and real yields and greater availability of foreign finance despite the persistent budget deficit overruns (the deficit outturns were consistently over 7% of GDP during 1995-1997).

Finally, by 1997 the attempts of the Russian government at credible stabilisation seemed to be paying off. The steady decline in M2 growth and inflationary expectations helped inflation fall to hitherto unseen levels – 48% in 1996 and 15% in 1997. Russia looked like it was on the road to recovery.

Monetary virtues and fiscal sins: The rude awakening of August 1998

The early years of reform were a process of learning the established maxim that inflation was essentially a monetary phenomenon and macroeconomic stabilisation involved above all the control of monetary emissions while output recovery could only be achieved by structural reform. What Russian policy makers did not understand or, in any case, did not act upon, was another simple principle of macroeconomics, namely that lasting stability could not be achieved alongside unsustainable levels of public debt. As Table 1 shows, the state stopped printing

---

[14] Clearly the markets expected a resumption of growth and higher future tax revenues. This helped Russia to switch to bond finance without having to face Sargent and Wallace's 'unpleasant monetary arithmetic'.

20

money by reducing the quantity of credit to the government, but continued to spend far in excess of its revenues, using domestic and foreign savings instead to finance the difference. This is a situation, which largely depends on confidence, a notoriously fragile commodity in emerging market finance. A series of unfortunate domestic and global events conspired to shatter confidence and led to the recent debacle.

The 1995-1997 period was a unique opportunity to pursue serious reform with the help of international finance. Budgetary reform and real restructuring could have been more gradual than otherwise, with a view of lessening the pain for ordinary people. Unfortunately the government failed to take advantage of the available opportunity and did not redress the fundamental problem of insufficient revenue collection. Instead it attempted to accumulate increasing amounts of debt, a dangerous Ponzi[15] game with investors, which they eventually refused to participate in.

What we need to consider next are the reasons for the collapse in the revenue collection capabilities of the Russian state, which lies behind the persistent fiscal imbalances of the last several years. A number of reasons emerge: quasi-fiscal subsidies to the industrial sector, chaotic intergovernmental relations, endemic tax evasion by the new private sector and rampant fiscal corruption.

---

[15] Ponzi was a 19th Century French financier who attempted to maintain a lavish lifestyle by accelerating his borrowing.

4. The Fiscal Collapse

It is a fairly uncontroversial view that the current crisis has its roots in the unsustainable nature of Russia's persistent fiscal imbalances. As such, the roots of the crisis are budgetary in their origin and hence any long-term plan for restoring stability in the country will have to redress Russia's persistent inability to collect taxes. Here we will attempt to give some explanation for the persistent failure of successive governments to increase tax revenues and achieve budget balance. In Chapter 3 we briefly touched upon the government's attempts to pressure the extracting monopolies for higher tax contributions. This chapter offers a more thorough analysis of the political economy of Russian fiscal arrangements.

Russia's 'Virtual Economy': budget offsets and the growth of barter

The term 'Virtual Economy' originates from the Karpov Report of December 1997. The aim of the study was to document and explain the staggering extent to which barter and non-payment of taxes and suppliers had become normality in Russia. Just a few numbers can reveal the degree of the problem. By May 1998 the net arrears of the industrial sector (the excess of overdue payables over overdue receivables) reached $60 billion (or approximately 15% of GDP!) of which wage arrears comprised $9 billion. The share of barter deals in industry surpassed 50% in 1998. In 1997 almost 40% of all taxes received by the federal government were in non-monetary form. Worse still, the Karpov report found that the average real value of the output supplied as barter payment is only one third of its nominal value indicating that in most cases barter is just another form of non-payment.

The main puzzle for those of us who have never run a Russian state owned enterprise is why supplies continue in the face of non-payment and why barter goods are accepted instead of cash when it is clear to everybody that they are not worth very much at all. Gaddy and Ickes (1998) offer a neat and convincing explanation, which is deeply embedded in the institutions and culture of the old command economy, that have been preserved until the present.

A brief detour: how industry in the command economy operated
Under socialism, an enormous expansion of industrial output took place, driven by state directed investment. The ideological drive to expand industry at all costs coupled with weak firm-level financial discipline (Kornai's 'soft budget constraint') led to the development of substantial chronic excess demand for productive factors. In order to keep fulfilling what was sometimes a very inconsistent plan, state firms had to develop an elaborate system of contacts with central government and other firms through which to obtain inputs and negotiate lower output targets. It was through good connections that quantity and plan-obsessed industrial enterprises were able to grow in size and prestige.

The 'business institutions' of the planned system continued to govern the relationships of state firms with the government and amongst themselves after the formal removal of central control. As the cost of inputs jumped to more realistic levels and unsold output stocks piled in the warehouses, manufacturing firms began making enormous losses. Some inevitable restructuring took place as production and employment was reduced. However, a surge in interenterprise arrears and a sharp fall in labour productivity also occurred, suggesting that state firms were delaying the necessary adjustments and were instead relying on credits from the CBR and other enterprises. The continued softness of budget constraints was operational due to the old connections of Soviet-era managers, who relied on the fact that a 'soft' central bank loan was only a phonecall away. Indeed the 'early reform efforts' of 1992–1995 were characterised by successive attempts to tighten monetary policy, which were abandoned by the government under pressure from the industrial lobby for liquidity in order to clear the stock of unpaid debts[16].

Such behaviour continued after the Gaidar mass privatisation programme of 1992. The latter was conceived as a political step, which was to privatise firms quickly to their managers and workers. The idea was that the collapse of the Soviet Union was a 'window of opportunity' to entrench market reforms and create sections of the populace who were in support of them. Almost overnight,

---

[16] See Skidelsky and Halligan (1996) for more details on the early reform efforts in Russia.

former state property became private and Russia was 'transformed' into a 'market economy'.

Although the Gaidar programme was well intentioned, it is fairly clear by now that in economic terms it was a dismal failure. There is a substantial body of empirical evidence, which suggests that outside control (i.e. neither by the workers nor by the managers) of enterprises is a necessary precondition for restructuring and efficiency gains. Selling state firms to strategic investors, who have the capital and the expertise, seems by far the best way to increase revenues, profits and, perhaps paradoxically, employment.[17] On the other hand, insider control is associated with falling labour productivity and very little restructuring. There are many possible reasons for such findings. Lack of managerial expertise is undoubtedly a leading factor. The Soviet era company directors, although good at extracting subsidies from the state, have not managed to adjust to the conditions of the market economy and find new products and buyers. Even if there were some who may have been willing to implement reforms, they would have been hampered by the lack of working capital, which is an endemic feature of the industrial sector in many transition economies. The poor legal framework and the weak protection for property rights make it highly unlikely that minority shareholders would invest in these newly privatised enterprises. The end result is a paralysis of the production process, a collapse in investment and a further deterioration in competitiveness.

Ironically, these failures of the newly privatised companies have created a strong lobby against reform – the

---

[17] Frydman et al. (1997)

exact opposite to what the architects of the programme intended. Unable and unwilling to change, the industrial sector and its political supporters have turned into a major obstacle to the structural reforms, which would threaten its survival.

Post-stabilisation adjustment: the 'Virtual Economy'

The continued survival of the unreformed industrial sector is central in explaining the persistence of Russia's fiscal problems in 1995-98. During this period, the Chernomyrdin administration finally found the political will to stop printing money and to tighten monetary policy. As a result inflation fell sharply, but inter-enterprise, wage and tax arrears rose (see Figure 3).

A simultaneous development was the sharp increase in barter transactions between enterprises, which surpassed 50% of all payments in 1998. Reliance on *veksels* (unit of account for barter transactions, which are mainly issued by the energy monopolies) has risen even for the payment of taxes to central and regional government. On the subject of such modes of exchange the Economist Intelligence Unit writes,[18] '...the use of *veksels* and other monetary surrogates is preferable to outright non-payment.' Such an argument seems innocuous enough. Even if the average *veksel* has a cash value of not more than one third of its nominal, some revenue is better than no revenue, and hence the reliance of barter at least does no harm to the economy.

---

[18] Country Report Series, Russia 2nd Quarter 1998.

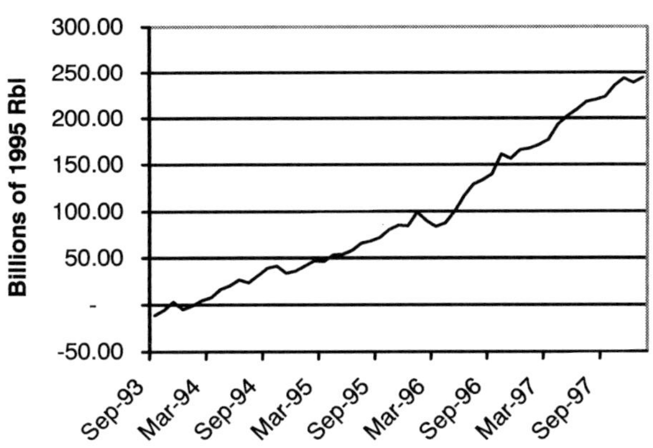

This would be true if the use of *veksels* was confined to the private sector, and thus the mutual provision of credit was a closed loop system. Unfortunately this is not the case. Barter instruments were used to pay primary input suppliers (such as profit making oil and gas companies[19]), who then used them to pay their taxes to the central government. The case of the Unemployment Fund of the Republic of El-Mari, discussed in Gaddy and Ickes (1997), provides a highly illustrative, if tragic, example. It received its Federal Government grant in the form of 10 tonnes of toxic chemicals from the Middle Volga Chemical Plant. The latter had offered the chemicals as tax payment

---

[19] An observer recently remarked that these sectors are perhaps the only value adding sectors in the Russian economy.

to the state, claiming that they were worth $80,000. Hence, the end providers of hidden subsidies to the inefficient manufacturers are the federal government, the value adding extracting monopolies and the workers whose wages have not been paid for months.

So why does everybody participate in this scheme to pump money into unviable Russian industry? Clearly the sector itself benefits since otherwise it would have to undergo much painful restructuring and its management will almost definitely be removed. The unpaid industrial workers also benefit from the *status quo*. The obvious reason for this is the unemployment situation in Russia. The ILO definition of the rate of joblessness reached 11.5% by the middle of 1998 and the rate of outflows from unemployment has been consistently very low since the beginning of the transition. Hence, the job prospects for any workers who lose their jobs at the present moment are very unfavourable indeed. Whatever little payment they receive from their 'day jobs' is better than nothing[20].

The extracting monopolies also benefit from the system, not least because they owe their existence to the politicians who support it. It is no secret to most Russians that the valuable state enterprises - those that control the

---

[20] Of course, the enterprise cannot completely stop paying its workers, since they would then leave no matter what their outside opportunities are. This 'cash constraint' determines how much of their output firms need to sell for cash in order to pay workers and how much they can barter at higher nominal 'prices'. Conditions in the wider economy (i.e. the prevailing wages and employment possibilities in the 'shadow economy') would tighten and relax this constraint as the firms strive to stop employees from leaving or starving.

nation's mineral reserves - have been handed out at knockdown prices to the political allies, personal friends and relatives of those in power. The former PM and Gazprom Chairman, Viktor Chernomyrdin, for example, is thought to have amassed an enormous personal fortune from various 'privatisation deals' involving oil and gas companies. Hence, although they can in theory refuse to supply non-payers and instead sell all their output in international markets for hard currency, Russia's extracting monopolies choose not to do so. They understand the need to support the weak and corrupt federal state, firstly, because they profit from its existence and its weaknesses and, secondly, because they fear the political consequences of its collapse. Hence the millions of dollars spent by Russia's 'oligarchs' in bankrolling Yeltsin's 1996 presidential campaign. A stronger personality at the Kremlin, the return to greater central control, and an end to the lucrative insider 'privatisations' was the last thing the financial elite wanted. An ailing and out of touch Yeltsin, entirely dependent on his advisers but occupying a post with huge constitutional powers, was in fact the best route to the capture and exploitation of the federal government for sectional interests.

The final player in the 'Virtual Economy' is the government. Without a coherent long-term strategy and lurching from one short-term policy measure to the next, the cabinets under Yeltsin seem to have 'stumbled' into lower inflation almost by accident. The willingness of the international community and the IMF to provide finance for Russia's restructuring helped the state to stop printing money without painful budgetary retrenchment, as did the emerging market investment boom of 1996-97,[21] which drove yields lower and reduced the cost of raising funds from capital markets. The result was the end of inflationary deficit financing and the beginning of the debt bubble. Impressed by Russia's success in reducing inflation, international investors piled into GKOs, confident that the budget would eventually be put in order. This, however, did not happen. None of the reformers such as Nemtsov or Chubais were willing or able to grasp the nettle of fiscal adjustment, which would have made them unpopular and destroyed their chances of succeeding Yeltsin after the year 2000.

A major reason for the state's ability to keep raising bond finance at falling interest rates was the country's rickety and corrupt banking system, which grew in 1994-95 on the vast profits from investments into short-term high-yielding sovereign bonds. Lacking the expertise and confidence to engage in lending to individuals and companies, Russia's private banks invested heavily into GKOs, driving interest rates down and making it cheaper for the government to issue them. Simultaneously, the fall in yields reduced the banks' profits per rouble invested and necessitated increased bond holdings to maintain profitability. Lacking the capital to do this, they borrowed heavily from western banks in foreign currency, betting on continued exchange rate stability.

This left the system in a state of precarious balance, which rested on continued foreign capital inflows and on the survival of the rouble's parity against the dollar. What brought its demise was the oil price collapse which

---

[21] The boom ended, of course, with the Asian collapse.

sent the balance of payments into deficit and the Asia-induced fall in foreign investor confidence, which started the selling of roubles and GKOs. Resting on the unsound foundations of federal deficits and an overvalued exchange rate, the 'Virtual Economy' could not withstand the pressure and after the loss of foreign reserves became unsustainable the rouble peg was abandoned and the financing of the internal debt suspended.

Tax sharing and the resurgent local government

The rising power of *oblast* and *krai* leadership has added another pillar in support of the perverse incentives facing the Russian industrial sector. Increasingly assertive regional leaders have claimed greater autonomy from Moscow including an increasing share of tax revenue. *Oblast* governments now receive almost half of the national tax take. Furthermore, regional authorities have taken the leading role in health and education expenditures as well as 'National Economy' spending (i.e. industrial subsidies).

This has had a double effect on the state enterprises within local jurisdictions. First of all, the source of cheap credits and outright subsidies has shifted and therefore the drastic reduction of subsidies at the federal level has not led to a fall in the total state support for industry.

To fund these new expenditures, *oblast* leaders have engaged in a murky and non-transparent negotiation game with the Moscow authorities over the division of locally collected revenues[22] between federal and regional level. This has resulted in a highly uneven and opaque distribution of resources, which is perceived as unfair (thus fuelling demands by those who feel left out) and which serves to undermine the centre's attempts to impose hard budget constraints on state firms as well as local governments.

Table 2: Regional and Federal Expenditures and Revenues: 1996–1997 (all figures in percentage of GDP)

1996	Health	Education	Social Policy	National Economy	Total Revenue	Tax Revenue
Regional	2.3	3.2	1.2	6	14.2	11.3
Federal	0.2	0.5	0.4	1.7	12.5	9.7
Total	2.5	3.7	1.6	7.7	26.7	21
1997						
Regional	2.5	3.5	1.2	6.2	15.3	12.3
Federal	0.3	0.6	0.9	1.8	12.8	9.1
Total	2.8	4.1	2.1	8	28.1	21.4

Source: Russian Economic Trends

To fund these new expenditures, *oblast* leaders have engaged in a murky and non-transparent negotiation game with the Moscow authorities over the division of

---

[22] Almost all revenues are now collected at the local level and then divided between Moscow and the collecting region according to a bilateral agreement. The lack of a universal tax sharing formula is creating much chaos and mutual discontent in inter-governmental relations.

locally collected revenues[23] between federal and regional level. This has resulted in a highly uneven and opaque distribution of resources, which is perceived as unfair (thus fuelling demands by those who feel left out) and which serves to undermine the centre's attempts to impose hard budget constraints on state firms as well as local governments.

Secondly, as local governments have acquired greater powers, they have increasingly lent a supporting hand to the structures of the 'Virtual Economy'. The volumes of non-cash tax contributions to *oblast* and *krai* authorities have surged since 1996 to reach 65% of the total[24]. Gaddy and Ickes tell the story of a hospital in the town of Kostroma, which when faced with a shortage of linens requested the local textile factory to deliver a certain quantity of its produce in lieu of its outstanding tax arrears to the local government. Why did the local authority not press the linen-maker to clear its arrears in the first place and then use the cash revenues to fund the hospital's needs? The answer is simple: because any receipt of taxes in cash has to be shared with the federal tier of government, whereas in-kind-payments do not. The local leadership then has every incentive to keep local enterprises under its control, that is, it would be opposed to any measures to privatise them. Also, it has an incentive to support

---

[23] Almost all revenues are now collected at the local level and then divided between Moscow and the collecting region according to a bilateral agreement. The lack of a universal tax sharing formula is creating much chaos and mutual discontent in inter-governmental relations.

[24] Quoted in S. Commander & C. Mumssen, (1998) 'Understanding Barter in Russia' EBRD Working Paper No. 37.

inefficient producers in order to extract payments in kind from them (which it does not share with Moscow) and then negotiate greater federal transfers in order to bail them out.

Many local officials have gone even further, acting as intermediaries between 'their' enterprises and the federal tax authorities in helping them to agree on tax offset schemes, whereby federal tax obligations (including obligations to social security and other funds) are cleared by barter contributions (see section on the 'Virtual Economy'). In addition, local organisations have been set up to engage in co-ordinating the complex barter transactions between enterprises. This reduces the costs of barter and facilitates a more efficient system of multilateral non-monetary exchange.

The biggest loser of such an arrangement is the federal government, which does not receive the taxes it would have collected under a cash-only system. Furthermore, restructuring and the resulting efficiency gains are obstructed by the local officials who would lose out from them.

Such perverse incentives are now thought to be very important in explaining both the growth of the barter-based 'Virtual Economy' and its resilience in the face of shocks. Moscow's concern with maintaining national unity by keeping separatist tendencies at bay, coupled with an anti-reformist Duma has made the task of facing up to regional interventionism an impossible one.

The growth of tax evasion and the shadow economy

The fact that the private sector does not pay its taxes is no secret to anyone with even a basic knowledge of the Russian economy. Estimates of the underground economy suggest that up to a third of economic activity goes unrecorded as business people strive to avoid the tax and regulatory burden imposed by the state. Enforcing tax-collection from such non-payers would substantially increase government revenues even if some marginal firms go bankrupt as a result. The questions which need to be addressed are: what drove the new private sector underground and what measures can bring it back into the official economy?

One of the most frequently cited explanations of the widespread tax-evasion is the hugely complicated and opaque tax system, which is used by corrupt tax-officials as a mechanism for bribe-extraction. Rather than try to comply with the numerous (and rapidly changing) taxes, fees and licenses, business people find it easier and cheaper to bribe officials.

A World Bank survey of Ukrainian entrepreneurs found that the average 'fee' paid to the tax inspector per quarter was $92 with 96% of respondents reported having to pay it. The total annual burden of official bribery was found to be $2,000 on average as opposed to the $12,000 required to operate legitimately. Figures for the Russian economy are unlikely to be much better. If anything, Russia's federal structure of government exposes businesses to the vagaries of multiple and inconsistent demands for taxes, regulatory requirements and other impediments to normal activity. Most entrepreneurs report that full compliance with these would drive them out of business.

The relationship between the citizen and the state is another very important factor leading to low tax collection in Russia. In most developed market-based democracies the state is organised as (more or less) a social contract which responds to popular demands and functions (again more or less) for the public good. Throughout Russian history this has never been the case. Until 1861 the vast majority of the population were serfs (i.e. little more than slaves). By the 1917 Revolution their position had improved on paper but not in reality. Poverty, war and bureaucratic terror periodically wreaked havoc in the lives of the illiterate and disempowered peasantry. Finally, the death of the Tsarist regime in 1917 marked the beginning of the most brutally oppressive political system in history.

The implications of such a history for private behaviour should be quite clear. The state is seen as the main enemy of the individual and hence 'shadow economy' activity is perceived as an essential method of survival. It would probably take generations and a substantial increase in political and economic freedom[25] for this relationship between the state and its citizens to change. Until then, underground activity and endemic private sector tax evasion will continue.

---

[25] A recent survey by Freedom House classified Russia as a 'partially free' country, thus falling short of a full democracy.

5. Turning back the Clock? Russia after August 17

The immediate consequences of the rouble devaluation appear to be two-fold: the loss of a framework for macroeconomic policy as well as the collapse in the post-1993 constitutional and informal power sharing arrangements.

The prospects for the economy

The end of 1998 and beginning of 1999 were characterised by the classical post-financial crisis phenomena of collapsing output, budget revenues and surging money supply growth.

The real economy

The sharp reversal in the current account which has swung into surplus in a matter of months has been achieved by a general reduction in domestic demand. This has manifested itself in a collapse of consumer spending hitting the new service sector of Moscow and the other big cities. Industrial output also fell sharply in the aftermath of the crisis as enterprises found it increasingly difficult to obtain imported (i.e. dollar denominated) inputs. Production volumes and composition have had to be modified accordingly to match the new cost and availability of foreign exchange. As a result, output has subsequently stabilised at a lower level, reflecting the new post devaluation cost and demand conditions in the economy.

To make matters worse, the last harvest has been one of the worst in living history. Anticipating shortages of basic foodstuffs in the winter food producers have been hoarding supplies, further worsening the situation in the cities and leading to some regional political tensions.

The banking sector has all but collapsed. Many of the biggest financial institutions who took part in the GKO bubble of 1996-1997 have now either closed or are heavily behind with their payments. The government has been engaged in murky negotiations trying to save the others while extending large quantities of central bank credit to keep them liquid. Indeed, credit to the financial sector accounts for much of the 25% expansion of the nominal base money stock since the end of August.

The state of government finances

The response of the Primakov government to the crisis has been one of generous promises and careful actions. During September he has declared his intentions to clear all state pension and wage arrears and pump money into the industrial sector in order to clear the vast stock of inter-enterprise debt. In reality, the cabinet has been heavily constrained by the collapse in fiscal revenues which in September were only half of the projected figure in the 1998 budget. Thus the government restricted itself to paying the overdue salaries of the armed forces and pensioners, reflecting concerns about the former's key role in preserving social order and the latter's special vulnerability in times of economic crisis.

In addition to the fall in revenues, Russia faces the need to begin servicing the GKO/OFZ stock after the three month moratorium expired in December. It is now clear that the state will have to also default on the restructured Soviet era debt - PRIN/IANs with large payments of both principal and interest in the middle of 1999 coinciding with due payments on Russian Eurobonds. Given the low foreign exchange reserves of the Central Bank and the reluctance of international lenders to commit more money to the black hole of Russian state finances, a full or partial default looks inevitable.

An external default will not, however, solve all the country's internal financing problems. The 1999 budget projects a consolidated government cash deficit of 6.25%. Given the insolvency of the Russian government it is unlikely that much non-inflationary finance would be forthcoming. According to calculations by the Institute for the Economy in Transition, the state will need seigniorage of between 2.8% and 3.6% of GDP (the budget assumes 3%). Given the demonetised state of the Russian economy, where rouble cash holdings account for only 2.5% of nominal GDP, such seigniorage needs will lead to three - or even four - digit inflation rates. Of course at such extreme levels of inflation the public's desire to hold cash balances will fall, further reducing the inflation tax base and necessitating an acceleration of the printing press. The end result would have to be stabilisation or hyperinflation. In short, one cannot hope to extract much monetary finance from a semi-barter economy.

What this means then is that slow payment and incomplete indexation alongside high inflation will serve as an implicit mechanism for cutting real expenditure and ensuring that seigniorage needs are smaller than those projected in the budget. Such 'unpleasant arithmetic' does not bode well for the living standards of ordinary Russians who are dependent on state salaries and social security payments.

Political developments

The rouble devaluation has brought about a political as well as an economic crisis in Russia. All confidence in the political elite's ability to lead the nation out of the current chaos has evaporated. The President is a shadow of his former self, utterly unable to yield the power which his own constitution bestows upon him. He has stepped down in all but name, already clearing the decks for the next presidential campaign.

The Government and the prime minister (and their backers in the Duma) are hesitantly taking on the leading role. Dominated by demagogues like Zhirinovsky and Ziuganov, the new 'coalition of despair' (comprising Communists and nationalists) both wants and fears power because it does not know what to do with it. They have no coherent economic programme apart from (deliberately) vague suggestions that 'controlled monetary emissions' should be undertaken in order to inject some liquidity into bankrupt banks and insolvent enterprises. Nobody is clear, however, about what is going to follow, including the 'programme's' architects themselves. That is

40

why the Communists have carefully distanced themselves from the Primakov government while making sure that their economic 'expert' Yuri Masliukov is in the cabinet. What they want is power (or influence) without responsibility, which can only be indicative of the widespread confusion and lack of confidence in the new government and the policies it is about to pursue. The government itself has acted less like an authoritative initiator of economic policies designed to lead Russia out of the crisis and more like a follower of the moods of the day, leaking vague proposals to the press in order to test the public reaction.

The main problem with the Communists is their inability to forge a new identity in the changed political and socio-economic conditions of today's Russia. The crash of the command model and the party's support of the failed 1993 coup have generated a huge credibility gap with the mainstream electorate. This has left the party no choice but to rely on its natural constituency, a coalition of the 'losers' from economic reform, including pensioners, the unemployed and army personnel, who are bitter about the fall in their living standards and prestige and are therefore very unwilling to relinquish their belief in the old Marxist-Leninist doctrines. Thus the Communists have fallen into the trap of relying on a large and potentially influential coalition of voters, which is, however, a backward looking one, and thus utterly incapable of offering a possible way forward. This has rendered the party unable to take the kind of tough decisions needed to get the country out of the current mess.

Similarly, the reformist camp appears to be in utter disarray. Divided and discredited due to the recent policy failures, it does not currently offer any serious political alternative to the nationalist-communist coalition.

The root cause of the recent political paralysis is the electorate's unwillingness to accept and understand the painful truth that the August crisis was the result of too little, rather than too much economic reform. The country's politicians have in turn responded by using the old rhetoric about Russia's special history and national character, which makes it unsuitable for rapid market reforms. Multi-ethnicity, the country's size and the inherent immorality of the ruling classes are only a few of the many excuses for abandoning the policy of hard money and sound government finance in favour of a 'more typically Russian' approach of profligate and short-termist 'controlled inflation'[26].

The political elite's inability to offer leadership has been met by the electorate with widespread apathy and cynicism about the ability of the political system to deal with the country's problems. Ordinary Russians have simply been stepping up efforts to stockpile food supplies for the winter and/or switch out of roubles and into dollars. The mood in the country is one of fear and concern rather than anger. People are not protesting, still in shock and confused about what is happening in their

---

[26] Note that 'controlled inflation' has recently been advocated as a method of getting Japan out of the liquidity trap it currently finds itself in. Since a liquidity trap is a situation whereby monetary policy loses its effectiveness as nominal interests rates fall to zero, this argument clearly does not apply to Russia where nominal and real interest rates are very high.

country. Yeltsin was the main hope of the forward-looking part of the population, who desired further moves towards a market economy. This was reflected in the overwhelming vote in his favour in 1996 and in the current state of depression and paralysis, which is gripping the nation. Until recently political choice was easy: one was either pro- or anti-Yeltsin. From now on, actual political choices have to be made.

Big uncertainties also lie with the power and influence of the men who have been ruling Russia in the past two years - the much-maligned 'financial oligarchs', who run the country's Financial and Industrial Groups (FIGs). Has the recent debacle weakened their power by bankrupting the banks they controlled and which served as the symbol of their financial might? It is too early to say. Large-scale Russian underworld capital flight has been an ongoing phenomenon of the last several years and it is difficult to imagine that the oligarchs (who presumably knew well the unsustainability of the economic situation) did not export most of their fortunes into the safe havens of Switzerland or Cyprus. Hence, if money buys power in today's Russia, and the oligarchs are still in possession of their financial wealth, then they should be able to exert considerable influence on any government. On the other hand, it is possible that the crumbling of their ostentatious displays of power - the flash new banks - will weaken the respect the oligarchs command in political circles. The present government appears to be bowing to some extent to pressure from the banks for liquidity, although there are few indications of a full-blown state bailout. The most likely final outcome is, of course, that some banks and oligarchs are saved and others (the ones with less political clout) will have to close.

Recent events seem to have definitely strengthened the hand of another lobby, that has been blamed for the current crisis - the former/present state owned industrial sector. The neo-communist swing back to forced sales of foreign exchange earnings to the CBR as well as the promises of money printing in order to support the economy are the sort of policies, which have long been advocated by the industrial lobby. However, since they have no funds to finance political campaigns and control media groups, the influence of the old state enterprise managers is only likely to last as long as the communist/nationalist resurgence.

The prospects for reform

In the longer term there are great uncertainties regarding Russia's constitutional arrangements and political climate. At present all the indications are that a resurgent Duma will try, and probably succeed in, amending the 1993 Constitution in order to strengthen the legislature *vis-à-vis* the President. Will this further impede the political system's capability for economic reform? Not necessarily, although, of course, the danger is always there. There is no reason why a parliamentary coalition cannot push reforms through in a similar manner to a President. Naturally, this requires strong and charismatic leaders as well as public interest in, and support for, economic reforms. It is the latter which is likely to be the main problem in a country tired of reforms (they haven't stopped since Gorbachev came to power in 1984) and desperate to see the long-awaited increase in living standards, which the market was supposed to bring. Only a serious deterioration in the economic climate (such as hyperinflation, for example) will bring about a shift in public opinion which is favourable to the implementation of a radical monetary and fiscal stabilisation programme[27].

The dangers with relying on big economic disruptions to provide the impetus for economic reform are all too obvious. Although the experience of hyperinflation in countries such as Argentina and Bulgaria led to large shifts in political opinion in favour of radical measures,[28] history is replete with sinister examples of social collapse or rightwing take-overs. Russia itself set off on the road to communism in 1917 amidst the huge economic and political crisis caused by the Tsarist government's handling of the First World War.

It is difficult to see who, in present day Russia, can provide the right mix of charisma and demagoguery needed to seize power. Crises, however, have the potential to create leaders as well as destroy them (remember Yeltsin's defiant stand against the 1991 coup attempt) and many of today's 'harmless eccentrics' (such as Zhirinovsky or Lebed) in Russia could turn out to be tomorrow's violent dictators. This is something liberally minded

---

[27] Current opinion polls suggest that up to 80% of Russians support price controls on certain commodities (such as food) and over 40% are in favour of restricted internal convertibility of the rouble. This obviously does not constitute support for market friendly stabilisation methods.

[28] Both countries adopted currency boards (Argentina in 1991, Bulgaria in 1997).

Russians and western governments need to bear in mind when formulating policy in today's turbulent times.

6. What Future for Russia?

Russia's fiscal problems are deeply embedded in an unreformed institutional framework, whose culture and origins date back to Soviet times and which has evolved to ensure its self-preservation. As such, it has both shaped and developed under the influence of the conditions of the Russian-style capitalism that has taken hold after the collapse of communism. The network of financial oligarchs, corrupt officials and politicians, gangsters and industrial managers all relentlessly pursue their own ends like they always have done, this time without the strong central restraining force which existed during the socialist era. Alongside them, the 150 million Russians continue their everyday struggle for survival involving small scale farming, tax evasion or belt tightening.

There will be no radical departure from this age-old social pattern either in the near, or more, distant future. What would make the difference between triumph and disaster is whether its socially and economically deleterious consequences are kept at a level which is sustainable in the long run. As the experience of 1997-1998 shows, if low inflation is to last, it would have to be accompanied by moves that reconcile budgetary and socio-political stability. This is indeed the greatest challenge of the transition project and it involves the meeting of many conflicting objectives. In the long-term, social stability and a sustainable national debt stock are best served by rapid economic growth. This, in turn, necessitates drastic improvements in the physical and social infrastructure in order to encourage the necessary quantities of foreign and domestic investment. Therefore, both the quantity and efficiency of the provision of essential public goods, such as law and order maintenance, needs to rise. And this requires, above all, a great improvement in the general quality of government.

Unfortunately, during the last several years government policy has not done enough in meeting this challenge. Instead, it has been driven excessively by powerful special interests towards the achievement of short term objectives. Hence, there are a number of policies the government must implement in order to redress this imbalance and relax its fiscal constraint. First of all, it ought to end the practice of short term social protection through the state support of uncompetitive and value-destroying economic activities. Instead, the task of compensating the losers from reforms can be assigned to a modernised system of social security provision which is much less distortive.

Secondly, changes in the way the centre and the regions share revenues and expenditures are long overdue. The present system encourages inefficient methods of in-kind tax payment, which impede restructuring, reduce total revenue and place a large fiscal burden on the federal level.

A third imperative is the 'renationalisation' of property rights protection. In most developed countries the enforcement of property rights and the rule of law is a public good provided by the state and paid for by general taxation. The effective protection of property rights in

Russia has become increasingly a private business with bodyguards, protection money to gangsters and the police increasingly used in conjunction with widespread bribery to buy peace of mind for business people. Squeezed from one side by organised crime and from the other by crippling taxes and corruption, it is little wonder that the Russian private sector does not pay its taxes. Many businesses would probably close if they did.

What is the likelihood, then, of the above policies being implemented? The optimistic scenario envisages long-lasting political damage to the Communists from the inflationary policies of the Primakov cabinet (or of any cabinet which replaces it) and the election of a considerably more pro-reform Duma, which will create another 'window of opportunity' for the implementation of (most of) the necessary economic changes. Within 2-3 years, as high inflation destroys the value of the GKO debt stock and those few savings which remain in the banking system, the state and the financial system would gradually move towards solvency. By then, the current political struggle would be resolved by elections and the interventionist instincts of left-leaning politicians would be silenced by the imperatives of meeting the conditions for IMF loans. Russia will stabilise (probably with the help of a currency board and large western loans) and set off on the road to the 'Promised Land' of economic recovery.

More realistically, Russia would continue making its stormy evolution from socialism to its own version of a market economy. A look at the history of most economies (and especially developing ones) reveals that fiscal problems and protectionist pressures hardly ever disappear. Russia is highly unlikely to be an exception to this general rule. Thus the crisis of August 1998 will not be the last. What matters much more, however, is whether the conditions for the prosperity of the new (foreign as well as domestic owned) private sector are put in place. The strengthening of the rule of law, the simplification of the tax system and a reduction in corruption are necessary. This will 'renationalise' private property protection and lay the foundations of a better relationship between business and the state. Once this is in place, Russia will even be able to start building a normal financial system and return to the international capital markets once again. Then, perhaps, the long awaited boom will come.

Bibliography

Bruno, M. (1993), *Crisis, Stabilisation and Economic Reform,* Oxford: Clarendon Press.

Bruno and Easterly (1996), 'Crises and Long-run Growth', IMF Working Paper.

Commander and Mumssen, (1998) 'Understanding Barter in Russia' EBRD Working Paper No 37.

Transition Report 1998, EBRD, London.

Economist Intelligence Unit, *Country Report Series,* Russia: 3rd Quarter 1998, 2nd Quarter 1998.

Frydman, R., C. Gray, M. Hessel, A. Rapaczynski (1997), 'Private Ownership and Corporate Performance: Evidence from Transition Economies', (available at http://www.stern.nyu.edu/~nroubini/asia/asiahomepage.html)

Gaddy, C. and Ickes, B. (1997), 'Beyond a Bailout: Time to face the truth about Russia's 'Virtual Economy'', available at http://www.stern.nyu.edu/~nroubini/asia/asiahomepage.html .

Krugman, P. (1979), 'A Model of Balance of Payments Crises', *Journal of Political Economy.*

Lieven, A (1998), 'History is not Bunk', *Prospect,* October.

Russian Economic Trends, April 1998 (database available from http://cep.lse.ac.uk/datalib/index.html)

Sargent, T. and Wallace, N. (1981), 'Some unpleasant monetarist arithmetic', *Federal Reserve Bank of Minneapolis Quarterly Review,* pp. 1-17.

Skidelsky, R. and Halligan, L. (1996) *Macroeconomic Stabilisation in Russia: Lessons of Reform, 1992-1995,* The Social Market Foundation, London.

Skidelsky, R. (ed.), (1998), *The Politics of Economic Reform,* The Social Market Foundation, London

Centre for Post–Collectivist Studies Publications

1. *Russia's Stormy Path to Reform*
Robert Skidelsky (ed.)
£20.00

2. *Macroeconomic Stabilisation in Russia:*
Lessons of Reform, 1992-1995
Robert Skidelsky, Liam Halligan

3. *The End of Order*
Francis Fukuyama
£9.50

4. *From Capitalism to Socialism*
János Kornai
£8.00

5. *The Politics of Economic Reform*
Robert Skidelsky (ed.)
£8.00

6. *The Rise and Fall of the Swedish Model*
Mauricio Rojas
£10.00

7. *Capital Regulation: For and Against*
Robert Skidelsky, Nigel Lawson, John Flemming, Meghnad Desai,
Paul Davidson
£10.00

SMF Publications

1. *The Social Market Economy*
Robert Skidelsky
£3.50

2. *Responses to Robert Skidelsky on the Social Market Economy*
Sarah Benton, Kurt Biedenkopf, Frank Field, Danny Finkelstein, Francis
Hawkings, Graham Mather
£3.50

3. *Europe Without Currency Barriers*
Samuel Brittan, Michael Artis
£5.00

Reports

1. *Environment, Economics and Development after the 'Earth Summit'*
Andrew Cooper
£3.00

2. *Another Great Depression? Historical lessons for the 1990s*
Robert Skidelsky, Liam Halligan
£5.00

3. *Exiting the Underclass: Policy towards America's urban poor*
Andrew Cooper, Catherine Moylan
£5.00

4. *Britain's Borrowing Problem*
Bill Robinson
£5.00

Occasional Papers

1. *Deregulation*
David Willetts
£3.00

2. *'There is no such thing as society'*
Samuel Brittan
£3.00

3. *The Opportunities for Private Funding in the NHS*
David Willetts
£3.00

4. *A Social Market for Training*
Howard Davies
£3.00

5. *Beyond Unemployment*
Robert Skidelsky, Liam Halligan
£6.00

6. *Brighter Schools*
Michael Fallon
£6.00

18.   *Setting Enterprise Free*
       Ian Lang
       £10.00

19.   *Community Values and the Market Economy*
       John Kay
       £10.00

Other Papers

Local Government and the Social Market
George Jones

Full Employment without Inflation
James Meade

Memoranda

1.   *Provider Choice: 'Opting In' through the Private Finance Initiative*
      Michael Fallon
      £5.00

2.   *The Importance of Resource Accoutning*
      Evan Davis
      £3.50

3.   *Why there is no time to teach: What is wrong with the
      National Curriculum 10 Level Scale*
      John Marks
      £5.00

4.   *All free health care must be effective*
      Brendan Devlin, Gwyn Bevan
      £5.00

5.   *Recruting to the Little Platoons*
      William Waldegrave
      £5.00

6.   *Labour and the Public Services*
      John Willman
      £8.00

7.   *Organising Cost Effective Access to Justice*
     Gwyn Bevan, Tony Holland and Michael Partington
     £5.00

8.   *A Memo to Modernisers*
     Ron Beadle, Andrew Cooper, Evan Davis, Alex de Mont
     Stephen Pollard, David Sainsbury, John Willman
     £8.00

9.   *Consevatives in Opposition: Republicans in the US*
     Daniel Finkelstein
     £5.00

10. *Housing Benefit: Incentives for Reform*
     Greg Clark
     £8.00

11. *The Market and Clause IV*
     Stephen Pollard
     £5.00

12. *Yeltsin's Choice: Background to the Chechenya Crisis*
     Vladimir Mau
     £8.00

13. *Teachers' Practices: A New Model for State Schools*
     Tony Meredith
     £8.00

14. *The Right to Earn: Learning to Live with Top People's Pay*
     Ron Beadle
     £8.00

15. *A Memo to Modernisers II*
     John Abbott, Peter Boone, Tom Chandos, Evan Davis,
     Alex de Mont, Ian Pearson MP, Stephen Pollard,
     Katharine Raymond, John Spiers
     £8.00

16. *Schools, Selection and the Left*
     Stephen Pollard
     £8.00

17. *The Future of Long-Term Care*
     Andrew Cooper, Roderick Nye
     £8.00

Hard Data

3.   *Universal Nursery Education & Playgroups*
      Andrew Cooper, Roderick Nye
      £5.00

4.   *Social Security Costs of the Social Chapter*
      Andrew Cooper, Marc Shaw
      £5.00

5.   *What Price a Life?*
      Andrew Cooper, Roderick Nye
      £5.00

Trident Trust/SMF Contributions to Policy

1.   *Welfare to Work: The* America Works *Experience*
      Roderick Nye (Introduction by John Spiers)
      £10.00

2   *Job Insecurity vs Labour Market Flexibility*
      David Smith (Introduction by John Spiers)
      £10.00

3.   *How Effective is Work Experience?*
      Greg Clark & Katharine Raymond
      £8.00

Stockholm Network

1.   *Millennium Doom: Fallacies About the End of Work*
      Mauricio Rojas
      £10.00